The Story of Passover for Children

By Rabbi Francis Barry Silberg
Illustrated by Stephanie McFetridge Britt

IDEALS CHILDREN'S BOOKS

Text copyright © 1989 by Rabbi Francis Barry Silberg
Illustrations copyright © 1989 by Ideals Publishing Corporation
All rights reserved.
Printed and bound in the United States of America.
Published by Ideals Publishing Corporation
Nashville, Tennessee

ISBN 0-8249-8309-2

he Hebrew people lived long, long ago in Egypt. They had lived in peace over 400 years until a wicked king, Pharaoh, made them slaves. Pharaoh forced them to make bricks which they used to build huge cities. He set cruel taskmasters over the Hebrews, and they became bitter and sad.

One day, wicked Pharaoh ordered that every Hebrew newborn baby boy be killed.

Not long after this order, a little boy was born to a family of the Hebrew tribe of Levi. His mother kept him hidden from the Egyptians for three months; she was very afraid he would be found and killed. To hide him, she made a basket of slime and pitch. She placed the baby inside and set it in the river. His sister, Miriam, hid among the bulrushes and watched over the baby day and night.

One day, Pharaoh's daughter came down to bathe in this river.
She spotted the basket and asked her servants to bring it to her.
When it was opened, she saw that the crying baby was a Hebrew;
she took him home with her and raised him as her own. She chose
a name for him which meant "Child of the Great River Nile."
She called the baby *Moses*. Moses grew up in Pharaoh's house,
but he longed to be with his own people.

One day, Moses saw an Egyptian kill a Hebrew slave. Moses was so angry that he killed the Egyptian and then ran into the wilderness of Midian. He was taken in by a family and became a shepherd.

While Moses was in Midian, Pharaoh died; but the children of Israel, the Hebrews, were still slaves. God heard their cries. He remembered His promise to their fathers Abraham, Isaac, and Jacob, that one day they would live in a land rich with milk and honey.

While Moses was tending sheep on a mountainside, an angel of the Lord appeared to him in a bush that burned but was not consumed.

The Lord said, "I have seen the tears and have heard the cries of my people in Egypt. Now, Moses, go and deliver them from the house of bondage!"

Moses was afraid. He was afraid that he could not do what God wanted him to do. But the Lord said, "I will be with you, Moses. Tell the children of Israel that the Lord God has sent you to free them."

So Moses went to Pharaoh and said, ''The Lord, God of Israel, has commanded that you let His people go free that they might hold a feast in the wilderness.''

But Pharaoh said, ''I do not know this Lord and I will not let Israel go.''

Pharaoh then caused the Hebrews to suffer even more.

Moses was eighty years old when he returned to Pharaoh. His brother Aaron went with him as his spokesman. Aaron took Moses's great staff and threw it upon the ground at the feet of Pharaoh's court magicians. They then threw their staffs upon the ground. The staffs of the magicians turned into serpents. But Moses's turned into an even greater serpent and swallowed up the others. But Pharaoh still would not let God's people go.

One morning, Moses and Aaron met Pharaoh at the river. Moses said, "If you do not obey the command of the Lord

and let the Hebrew slaves go, the Lord will turn the river's water into blood.''

But Pharaoh's heart was hardened against the Hebrews. So Moses caused the staff to touch the water, and the water turned to blood. The fish swimming in the river died. The Egyptians became frightened and thirsty and feared the power of the Lord. But once again Pharaoh refused to let God's people go.

Then God sent frogs to Egypt. The frogs were everywhere—in the ovens, in the houses, in the streets. They covered the land. Pharaoh called Moses and begged him to stop the frogs. Pharaoh promised that if the Lord would take away the frogs, he would free the Hebrews.

God listened to Moses. But as soon as Pharaoh saw that the frogs had disappeared, he would not let the people go.

The Lord was angry. He commanded Moses to again stretch out his staff. Now gnats came to torment the Egyptians.

Pharaoh's magicians cried out to him, ''This is the finger of God!'' But Pharaoh still would not let the people go.

Moses told Pharaoh that God would send flies to Egypt. Pharaoh did not listen and the flies came. But the land where the Hebrews lived was spared. In this way, God showed that the Hebrews were His chosen people.

Pharaoh called out to Moses, asking him to speak to the Lord to end the flies. Moses warned Pharaoh that if Pharaoh once again

broke his promise and did not let the people go, Egypt would suffer more. The Lord listened to Moses and the flies left, but Pharaoh again refused to let the people go.

Then the Lord sent a plague on Egypt's cattle; all the horses and camels and flocks of sheep died. But not one of the Hebrews' animals died. Still Pharaoh would not let the slaves leave.

Next, the Lord sent boils to the skins of the Egyptians. They became very sick.

Then the Lord commanded Moses to raise his staff toward Heaven. As he did so, the Lord sent hail and fire. The land was burned, and the houses of the Egyptians were crushed. But the land and houses of the Hebrews were untouched.

Pharaoh pleaded with Moses to end the plagues saying that now he and his people had seen the power of the Lord. So God stopped the plagues. But again Pharaoh would not free the Hebrew slaves.

Soon Egypt was filled with locusts devouring the fields and fruit. Still, the people were not set free. Then God sent darkness to the land for three days. Pharaoh still would not free the Hebrews.

The Lord then told Moses that He would send one more plague. This would be a plague so terrible that Pharaoh would let the Hebrews go.

The Lord instructed the Hebrews that on the fourteenth day of the month called Nisan, they were to sacrifice lambs without any blemish. The Lord said they were to take the blood of the lambs and wipe it on the side posts of their doors. The Lord told them to roast the flesh of the lambs and to eat it with unleavened bread and bitter herbs. That night the Lord would pass over the bloodstained houses of the Hebrews, but He would stop at the houses of the Egyptians.

At midnight the Lord moved, and there came a great cry in the land. Every firstborn person and animal of Egypt died, but not one of the Hebrews or their animals. Pharaoh pleaded with Moses to go and take his people from Egypt.

Moses and the Hebrews left Egypt with their flocks and all their possessions. They left in such haste that the dough for their bread hadn't time to rise. So they baked unleavened cakes called matzah to take with them on their journey.

On that day, the Lord commanded the children of Israel to observe His Passover in every generation. He told them to remove

all leaven from their houses. He told them to eat unleavened bread for seven days. He told them to celebrate a feast on the first day and on the seventh day of the Passover observance. Then His people would never forget that the Lord had passed over their houses on that terrible night when He came to slay every firstborn in Egypt.

The children of Israel had lived in the land of Egypt for 430 years. Now, after the night of watching the Lord's passing over, they were free to worship the Lord. And the happy children of Israel followed Moses into the wilderness.